Aaron Rodgers

by Mari Schuh

Consultant: Barry Wilner
AP Football Writer

BEARPORT
PUBLISHING

New York, New York

Credits

Cover and Title Page, © Mike Roemer/AP Images and G. Newman Lowrence/AP Images; 4, © Ffooter/Shutterstock Images; 5, © Allen Fredrickson/Icon SMI; 6, © David Stluka/ AP Images; 6–7, © Mike Roemer/AP Images; 8, © ChameleonsEye/Shutterstock Images and Rafael Ramirez Lee/Shutterstock Images; 9, © Jeffrey Phelps/AP Images; 10, © Seth Poppel/Yearbook Library; 11, © Chico Enterprise-Record; 12, © Mike Roemer/AP Images; 12–13, © Chico Enterprise-Record; 14, 14–15, © Michael Pimentel/Icon SMI; 16, © Julie Jacobson/AP Images; 17, © Morry Gash/AP Images; 18–19, © Allen Fredrickson/Icon SMI; 20, © Aaron M. Sprecher/Icon SMI; 21, © Robin Alam/Icon SMI; 22, © Allen Fredrickson/ Icon SMI.

Publisher: Kenn Goin
Senior Editor: Joyce Tavolacci
Creative Director: Spencer Brinker
Photo Researcher: Arnold Ringstad
Design: Emily Love

Library of Congress Cataloging-in-Publication Data

Schuh, Mari.
  Aaron Rodgers / by Mari Schuh.
     p. cm. — (Football stars up close)
  Includes bibliographical references and index.
  ISBN 978-1-61772-714-6 (library binding) — ISBN 1-61772-714-8 (library binding)
 1. Rodgers, Aaron, 1983—Juvenile literature. 2. Football players—United States—
Biography—Juvenile literature. I. Title.
  GV939.R6235S38 2013
  796.332092—dc23
  [B]
                                    2012039651

For more information, write to Bearport Publishing Company, Inc., 45 West 21st Street, Suite 3B, New York, New York 10010. Printed in the United States of America.

10 9 8 7 6 5 4 3 2 1

Contents

Time to Shine

It was December 2008. **Quarterback** Aaron Rodgers glanced up at the scoreboard. His team, the Green Bay Packers, was beating the Detroit Lions 24–21 in the fourth quarter. If the Packers scored again, they would have enough points to almost guarantee a win. Aaron knew he had to make a move. So he took the **snap**, saw his teammate Donald Driver far down the field, and hurled the ball long and high. Was Aaron's throw good enough to help his team win the game?

The Green Bay Packers play home games in Green Bay, Wisconsin. Their stadium is called Lambeau Field.

LAMBEAU FIELD

Lambeau Field

Aaron manages to throw the ball seconds before being tackled during the December 2008 game against the Lions.

The Long Pass

Excited Packers fans watched as the ball soared across the field right into Donald's arms. After catching the ball, Donald bolted to the end zone for a **touchdown**. Aaron had thrown a 71-yard (65 m) touchdown pass! He smiled as the crowd went wild. It was only Aaron's first season as the Packers' **starting** quarterback. Fans wondered what else this talented quarterback had in store.

Donald Driver (#80) catches Aaron's pass before running for a touchdown.

Aaron (right) and Donald celebrate after working together to score a touchdown.

Aaron waited three years to become the Packers' starting quarterback. He had been the **backup** to superstar player Brett Favre.

Young Fan

Football had been a huge part of Aaron's life from a young age. He was born on December 2, 1983, in Chico, California. Aaron's dad had played **semiprofessional** football. Aaron often played catch with his dad and would try to perfect his throwing by tossing footballs through a tire swing. Watching him practice, Aaron's dad clearly saw that his son had found the sport he loved.

Aaron worked on his passes by throwing a football through a tire.

Aaron sometimes still plays baseball for fun.

Aaron also played baseball, soccer, and basketball, but football was his favorite sport.

High School Star

When it was time for high school, Aaron knew he wanted to continue playing football. By his junior year at Pleasant Valley High School in Chico, California, Aaron was the star quarterback. The team did not win many games, but Aaron's skill and passion were obvious. During his senior year in 2001, he broke school records for passing yards and touchdowns.

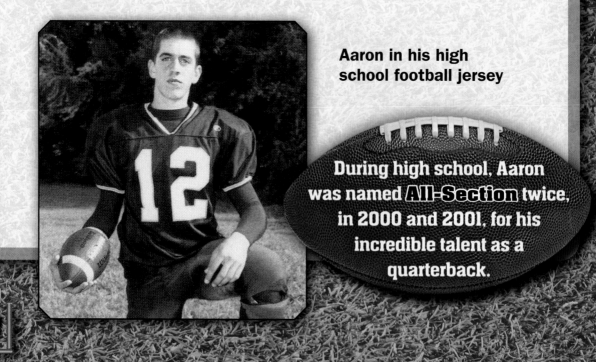

Aaron in his high school football jersey

During high school, Aaron was named **All-Section** twice, in 2000 and 2001, for his incredible talent as a quarterback.

Aaron scrambles away from a tackler during a high school game.

Small Beginnings

After his impressive high school career, Aaron had hoped that colleges with great football programs would offer him a **scholarship**. However, none of them did. Even though Aaron had been a star player, many colleges overlooked him because his high school team wasn't strong. When a small school in California called Butte Community College asked Aaron to play for them, he quickly accepted.

Aaron wearing a Butte Community College sweatshirt at a press conference

During a Butte football game, Aaron (#4) looks downfield for an open receiver.

Aaron played at Butte Community College for one year. His 28 touchdown passes shattered the school's old record.

A New College

At Butte, Aaron's ability to throw the ball long and accurately attracted the attention of coaches from major football colleges. His strong season earned him a football scholarship to the University of California at Berkeley (Cal), where he continued to impress. His 19 touchdown passes—and very few **interceptions**—in his first year dazzled fans. Aaron soon set his sights on playing in the **NFL**.

Aaron throws a pass in a 2004 game at Cal.

Aaron celebrates with fans after winning a game at Cal.

In 2004, his second year at Cal, Aaron led the team to a spectacular 10-1 record.

Drafted

In 2005, before his senior year at Cal, Aaron left college to enter the NFL **draft**. He hoped a team would pick him right away. When the Green Bay Packers didn't choose him until near the end of the first round, Aaron was very disappointed. The Packers already had one of the best quarterbacks in NFL history, Brett Favre. With Brett as the team's starting quarterback, Aaron knew that he would get few chances to play.

Aaron holds up a Green Bay Packers jersey.

Aaron works out with Brett (right) in early 2008.

Aaron played in only three games in his first year as a Packer. He threw just 16 passes and scored no touchdowns.

Aaron's Turn

Aaron waited for three years to be the Packers' starting quarterback. Finally, in 2008, Brett retired from the NFL. Packers fans loved Brett, but it was time for a new quarterback to take the field. Aaron quickly showed that he was ready to play hard, throwing an amazing 28 touchdowns in his first full season. Aaron was off to a great start, but he was just getting warmed up.

Brett Favre later changed his mind about retiring. He played for the New York Jets in 2008 and the Minnesota Vikings in 2009 and 2010.

Aaron throws a pass during his first season as a starting quarterback.

Aaron runs with the ball during a 2008 game.

Super Bowl Champ

Each year, Aaron got better and better. He led the Packers to the **Super Bowl** after the 2010 season. His precise passing and strong leadership helped the Packers beat the Pittsburgh Steelers 31–25. Aaron was also named Super Bowl **MVP**. In 2011, Aaron had his best season yet, setting a team record with 45 touchdown passes and leading the Packers to an amazing 15–1 record. His NFL career got off to a slow start, but Aaron Rodgers has shown he's a true NFL superstar.

Aaron holds up the Super Bowl trophy after the Packers beat the Steelers.

Aaron spots a receiver downfield during the Super Bowl in 2011

Aaron volunteers to help children who are sick. He also raises money to help scientists find cures for cancer.

Aaron's Life and Career

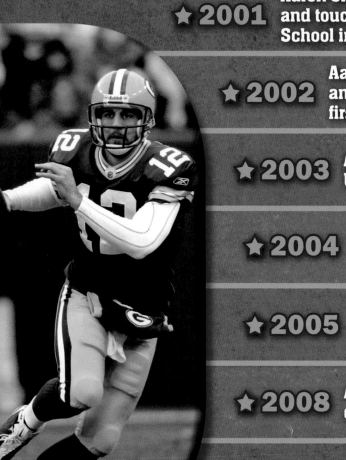

★ **December 2, 1983** Aaron Rodgers is born in Chico, California.

★ **2001** Aaron breaks school records for passing yards and touchdowns at Pleasant Valley High School in Chico, California.

★ **2002** Aaron attends Butte Community College and throws 28 touchdowns during his first and only year there.

★ **2003** Aaron begins playing for the University of California at Berkeley.

★ **2004** Aaron leads his team to a 10–1 record in his second year at Cal.

★ **2005** Aaron is picked by the Green Bay Packers near the end of the first round of the NFL draft.

★ **2008** Aaron becomes the starting quarterback for the Packers.

★ **2010** Aaron leads his teammates to the playoffs after a strong season.

★ **2011** Aaron leads the Packers to a Super Bowl victory and is named Super Bowl MVP.

Glossary

All-Section (ALL-SEK-shun)
a player named as one of the best
in a group of school teams

backup (BAK-uhp)
a player who doesn't play at the
start of a game and often doesn't
play at all; the second-best player
in a position

draft (DRAFT)
an event in which professional
football teams take turns choosing
college athletes to play for them

interceptions (in-tur-SEP-shuhnz)
passes caught by defensive players
on the other team, rather than
the offensive players they were
intended for

MVP (EM-VEE-PEE)
letters standing for the most
valuable player, an award given to
the best player in a game or in a
season

NFL (EN-EFF-ELL)
letters standing for the National
Football League, which includes
32 teams

quarterback (KWOR-tur-bak)
a football player who leads the
offense, the part of a team that
moves the ball forward

scholarship (SKOL-ur-ship)
an award that helps pay for a
person to go to college

semiprofessional
(SEH-mye-pro-fesh-uhn-uhl)
playing football for money but not
as a full-time occupation in the NFL

snap (SNAP)
the quick passing of the football to
the quarterback that starts a play

starting (START-ing)
being the coach's first choice to
play in a game

Super Bowl (SOO-pur BOHL)
the final championship game in the
NFL season

touchdown (TUHCH-*doun*)
a score of six points, made by
getting the ball across the other
team's goal line

Index

Bibliography

Gulbrandsen, Don. *Green Bay Packers: The Complete Illustrated History*. St. Paul, MN: MBI (2007).

Official Site of the Green Bay Packers: www.packers.com

Official Site of the NFL: www.nfl.com

Read More

Hoblin, Paul. *Aaron Rodgers: Super Bowl MVP (Playmakers).* Minneapolis, MN: ABDO (2012).

MacRae, Sloan. *Aaron Rodgers (Sports Heroes).* New York: PowerKids (2012).

Savage, Jeff. *Aaron Rodgers (Amazing Athletes).* Minneapolis, MN: Lerner (2012).

Learn More Online

To learn more about Aaron Rodgers, visit
www.bearportpublishing.com/FootballStarsUpClose